THE SPIRITUAL PILLAR *Of* LIFE

Unlock the gateway to your soul

By
MICHAEL ALAN SHEFFIELD

The spiritual pillar of life, unlock the gateway to your soul

Michael Alan Sheffield

COPYRIGHT 2023 © Michael Alan Sheffield

ISBNs
979-8-9876267-0-2

No part of this book may be copied or used without written permission from Author

DEDICATION

This book goes out to all the people that died trying to transcend to a higher frequency and to all the people that died without an understanding of this simulated reality also I want to dedicate this book to The Anunnaki Nibiru 12th Planet 9th Dynasty

Enki
Enlil
Anu
Marduk

I LOVE YOU ALL THANK YOU FOR THIS
Supreme-being knowledge

I ALSO WILL LOVE TO GIVE
A special dedication to My brother in the Cosmos
DARRYL LEE CHRISTMAS LOVE YOU BRO!

A DEDICATION TO MY FAMILY MEMBERS THAT
Transition to a higher frequency we love you

THANK YOU TO ALL THE PEOPLE THAT
Believed in me and still do I love you all

The supreme dedication to the highest the Supreme Universal energy I love you, thank you for always being with me and creating me.

CONTENTS

ACKNOWLEDGMENTS ... vii

CHAPTER 1: FREQUENCIES OF THE LIONS GATE ... 1

CHAPTER 2: A MESSAGE TO ALL LIGHT WOKERS ... 7

CHAPTER 3: FROM CONSCIOUSNESS TO ASCENSION ... 11

CHAPTER 4: DRACOS AND REPTILIANS LEARN THE HISTORY ... 19

CHAPTER 5: ELON MUSK IS TRYING TO TAKE OVER THE WORLD AS A DRACO REPTILIAN ... 27

ACKNOWLEDGMENTS

I would like to take this time to give thanks to Nibiru the 9th Dynasty the 12th Planet, in 2006 I was introduced to Nibiru by one of the greatest ascended masters of all time, magenta pixie. Once I learned about Nibiru My Life changed my eyes woke up, and I no longer was in the same reality, my mental perception changed.

I quickly started transcending from a 3D body two a 4th Dimensional light body my eating habits changed, I no longer craved flesh I stop eating chicken and beef. I started eating only fruits and vegetables, and I started studying and learned That fruits and vegetables have frequency codes of Light, once ingested into one's body they turn into downloaded messages that can be decoded into thoughts And reasoning.

I went to sleep one night woke up started studying saw a YouTube video it was a man by the name of Burt Goldman he showed me how to Quantum jump I realized the state of mind I was in everything became Clear, at the time I was sitting in my room that was my present reality. That week I set up a trip to Florida. That night I was sitting in my hotel room and suddenly I started thinking about Quantum Jumping.

I was in a whole new reality just by sitting in a different room, in a different place at a different time. I started to visualize my going back to my previous reality, But in the previous reality, I was able to change things before going back. At that moment I realized the art of Quantum Jumping and its power of it. Right after that, my life changed.

I had a dream that I was in Hong Kong. I visualized myself being there, I got invited in 2015 and Stayed there for four years. I started studying chakra points around the world I was attracted to a certain chakra point called **Uluru, or Ayers Rock the Solar Plexus Chakra of Earth [Uluru, A.K.A. Ayer's Rock.** My attraction to this chakra point became stronger every day, until one day I decided to go. I met the Aborigines of Australia,

I had a wonderful time.

I felt the energy from the chakra point. We stayed the week in Alice Springs Australia and got back to Hong Kong, One night I had a mental download. I learned about the Mayans' synchronized timeline, and I started studying my Galactic signature, 1320 Galactic Time synchronization that night I learned the quantum power of The Matrix, and I had a clear understanding of the power of numbers, and How they turn into Frequency, as I kept studying I learned about My kin number A frequency code attached to my magnetic codon.

I learned that being born on December 22 my birth month makes me an Ascended master that represents the four master numbers 11,22,33,44. Woke up the next day and my mental perception changed and was upgraded My DNA was different. My spirit felt freer than ever before. I started studying about the Anunnaki Tapped into the galactic codon Opened up a frequency of communication The knowledge I learned is extraordinary came back to America in 2019 I opened the portal to the 13th Gateway.

This Forbidden Knowledge started to spread to the Galactic Federation of Light to all the start seeds and all the light workers, As the knowledge started to spread we notice the polarized shift a lot of Souls and spirits started to ascend to a higher frequency to this day we continue to spread love knowledge and wisdom amongst each other worldwide and Beyond.

On my journey, I became the king of Finance for the tunnmma royal dynasty and the Anamase kingdom My name was Change the represent the new energy of life that I now hold I 'am HRH KING NII KENKEENFIOR RENICARNATED I would like to give a Special acknowledgment to

MY MOM IS VANESSA ENGLISH, MY DAD IS DARRYL SHEFFIELD MY BROTHERS NII AYITEY ANUMLE OYANKA, LAREMY WADE, RASHEED RAHAN WONDER SR, ERIC ACKILN, DAVONNE MOBLEY, AND ASAPH WOMACK

CHAPTER 1

FREQUENCIES OF THE LIONS GATE

Beloved Ones, At a time when we are still working on reclaiming our sovereignty; and hence freedom, towards the many manipulations that exist in our 3D matrix, we are being hit by Solar waves that are translated in our human view as heat ones, even in the countries where it is winter now. We need to understand that beyond our perception of what may cause these heat waves, lies the solar codes together with the Lions Gate frequencies.

That may be felt incredibly strongly in our bodies, but they are the ones that trigger the necessary shift that needs to occur for us to continue with the transformation that we have consciously chosen. Our family from Andromeda is masters in the art of adapting to change, for it is what we have agreed when we signed up for this experience, are helping many of us who wish to co-create with these benevolent beings to integrate these Current energetic waves, as they trigger the integration of such an amount of light, that we may not know how to properly direct towards our bodies.

These solar/heat waves are meant to help us open our heart center, for many are still in the midst of a profound heart healing, release old energies and embody a more illumined frequency by first burning what vibrates in a different density, which is achieved through DNA healing and reconnection, and by helping us build our light, bodies. It is very important to work on purification and stabilization to be able to be balanced as we continue embodying a new frequency and getting accustomed to how this new energy works.

When integrating this massive wave, we need to direct it with plenty of pure water and with our conscious decrees, integrating them gradually, and utilizing one of the most effective, in my personal experience, purification tools - seventh violet flame and White one = to help the bodies release and continue the process of embodiment. Having an excess of energy is not beneficial for our bodies, as when this occurs body anxiety takes place.

We may feel nausea, headaches, an internal feeling of being uncomfortable in our bodies, and many other personal sensations that will be unique to every one of us.

This means the nervous system and spinal cord have been affected and then we need to begin the process of body reconfiguration at all levels, especially upgrading our nervous system. When the nervous system and the spinal cord are affected, the body conduits for us to communicate with our soul and Unified Self are temporarily interrupted, and we need to manage energy properly and utilize it to locate within our template the parts of us that need healing. and restoration, dissolve any misalignment and stabilize all body centers again, so our bodies can come back to normal. Guides invite us to work with a sacred symbol, the Infinity one, to anchor and allow these energies to come into our bodies.

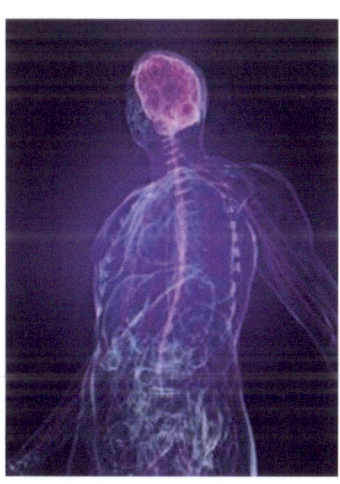

As I always say, our Unified Self will determine how much light we are ready to integrate, for the body could collapse, if we have not yet prepared it correctly. As you anchor and work with this symbol, you will begin to notice the wisdom - light - that begins to run through your body.

Guides also offer us a crystal to work with at this time, to be able to integrate the guidance, wisdom, and power that are coming from this massive wave, a Seraphinite. This crystal is to help us integrate our angelic and hence, sixth-dimensional frequency, as well as open our grown chakra, so the information can continue descending upon us. It is à natural balancer, and for those who are working with their shoulder wings portals, it will too help them reclaim their wings and authentic essence.

These are the natural effects of intentionally integrating the current energies. It is an organic process that when we see it as part of our ascension transformation, gets easier to assimilate, as we continue knowing our bodies and what they need when they shift massively.

Take good care of yourselves, beloved ones. Remember that we chose to experience this process and that when we know how our bodies work, and how to move our Consciousness through our bodies, we can make this process a more soothing one. Within Infinite Love, By Natalia Alba ~ Next Message Archangel Michael: Your Time Draws Near I am Archangel Michael with a message for the Angelic Warrior Group. Your time draws near. We are getting close to our first big win. However, this will not be our last challenge, not by far.

There will be more challenges in the future - more changes we need to make to reflect the truth of God's love for humanity on earth. Many more challenges. Your world must do an about-face. And it starts with the mind. Spend more time learning to accept, and spend more time learning to have compassion for others. Do not only focus on your benefit but ask what the world would look like if all were to benefit. Eliminate within yourself any resistance you may have to see others thrive as well, remembering that you are all One with God, and when others thrive, so do you.

This is true equality, not the disparity that you are taught is your cross to bear now. We have many still to rescue, those unknown faces that live within the bases, and those unknown hearts you have never come to know. Many on other planets have been trafficked and many who did not survive must be mourned by the others. There is much work to do and it must come from the heart now or it will not come at all.

This week we ask you to focus on the administration currently in charge of the United States. If you prefer focus your loving energies on the administration that currently governs your own country. If they have capitulated they will appreciate your support, but if they have not they will learn to fear the mind of the human as it is by far stronger than their own.

This will lead to further changes in their plans and further capitulation of those already on the fence. You will be aiding the Light forces in creating change on planet Earth and we thank you. I am Michael. I am your leader. I am your brother. We are Legion Adonai.

CHAPTER 2

MESSAGE TO ALL LIGHT WORKERS

As you have been told so often "There is only one!" This is an impossible concept for you to understand as humans in form, living in an unreal dream/nightmare environment that appears to you to be intensely and unalterably real, firm, and, solid. But it is true, and at the depths of your being, behind the veil or mist that you have placed between your true or higher selves and your egos, you do know and can access this divine truth.

Take time out at least once daily and set the intent very firmly and positively to access this deep and true inner knowing, and then relax. Totally - Without expectation - thus allowing your higher selves to reveal themselves to you through your inner knowing, your divinely given intuition. When you wait impatiently and expectantly, you give away your power to your egos, and they will always lead you away from Truth, away.

From M/F/G, insisting that you are wasting your time, that you are far too busy, and that you have a life to live, and thus you need all your energy for practical things with which your human lives need to be fully engaged. But, there are no things! There is only life, consciousness, awareness, Love, Source, M/F/G, and the ONE! So, being one, what do you need to do?

Nothing! You need, in every moment, to BE I that is your only task -to BE.

You are divine, you are one with Source, you are Love, and there is nothing else and no need for anything else because LOVE is ALL that Is! By trusting M/F/G and accepting yourselves, the divine and perfect children of God that you all are, as sinless and infinitely worthy of God's love, you are being your true selves - All that you can be pa, ALL - and your very presence in form NOW is strongly and most vigorously assisting in bringing The collective awakening into bloom.

That is precisely why you chose to be incarnate at this particular moment in humanity's irreversible spiritual evolution, while also accepting that while in the form you would indeed forget who you truly were, but would nevertheless follow a particular personal path through the illusion to assist in bringing about the collective awakening.

This - the collective human awakening - is happening now, at incredible speed and there are extremely clear signs of this wherever you choose to focus your human attention. Be of good cheer, all is well, It cannot be otherwise. You are doing what you are incarnated to do, you are being. Is being Love, which is your real and true nature. You cannot be anything other than Love, although as humans in form, in an unreal and very temporary environment, you can, and mostly do, choose to believe that the environment in Which you find yourselves is a totally real and often dangerous one, and so you mostly use or engage with your egos to guide and protect you from the dangers with which human life presents you, believing that to be loving is weak and will encourage others to take advantage of your weakness. And this mightily distracts or discourages you from being - you just don't seem to have the time! And yet you can't be remembered.

It was by your own free will choice that you incarnated, knowing that it was a most loving and courageous choice to make, and here you are seemingly lost and confused as you search for your life's purpose = to gain security, money, safety, love? - And in the end, none of those, even if achieved, serve to satisfy you. How could they? Only reawakening into your true state of Oneness with M/F/G MOTHER FATHER GOD- Love, capital L will bring you true peace and joy. Be fully aware that: You are here purely to awaken, and to help all those with whom you interact in any manner at all to awaken with you. That is your task, your purpose, and you are carrying it out, magnificently even though it is not apparent to you, either because you are getting practically no positive feedback about your most amazing achievements, or because you are not paying enough attention as your human lives in Form demand all of it.

Truly you are, every single human in form without any exceptions, the most magnificent and wonderful beings working in the dark = and without a flashlight - to bring all to the Light, and you are succeeding. Failure is not an option, it is impossible! Humans everywhere are about to have a collective awakening into full conscious awareness of each of their individual and most beautiful creative states of brilliance as One with Source, eternally in that Presence.

Our emphasis However, your free will is also an eternal gift from God to use whenever and however you choose; it will never be overridden. Therefore there will be some who make a completely incontrovertible choice to remain in the unreal state which humanity has been experiencing for eons of time. Those highly personal and individual choices will be fully honored for as long as those choosing to remain in unreality. For them, life will continue "as normal." However, those choices will not affect your collective awakening, because, by those very choices, they will be choosing to remain behind in an environment of fear, the state in which it seems that their survival is under almost constant threat, and in which it appears that conflict is an essential aspect of survival with which they have to engage constantly to ensure their ongoing existence as humans, the only form of life which they can conceive. When they finally and fully realize the insanity of almost constant open conflict, they too will awaken; with great exhilaration, into the joy of that eternal Presence in the One. Al is one, so not even one will be excluded because then the One would be Incomplete a total impossibility. Your loving brother, Ascended Master number 22.

CHAPTER 3

FROM CONSCIOUSNESS TO ASCENSION

The event and the grand solar flash - pleiadian light forces transmissions. a special message to the star seeds of the new earth, for immediate planetary broadcast.. Prelude: great one, the Pleiadians are masters of light, consciousness, and ascension and are indeed the benevolent watchers over the evolution of humankind! They speak higher truths, clearly to humans, in a down-to-earth and easy-to-understand way! The information they bring is pure light and is encoded in such a way as to activate dormant DNA strands and increase consciousness levels! There is nothing more true than what is and this higher light we speak of is eternal universal akashic data and is the ultimate truth! When this light comes into, the body, things start to activate: and turn on! This new light data triggers cellular DNA and causes much larger or more complex streams of cosmic-level information to flow through the DNA strands or optics of the body! this new higher data then becomes available to consciousness, greatly expanding awareness and levels of knowing! Furthermore, when this high-vibrational cosmic light data Begins to flow through the body, it unlocks memories stored in the cells of the body, even ancient memories! When all of this happens, one will experience an amazing, blissful aha moment where everything will begin to make complete sense, for the first time! At this point, all states of amnesia and ignorance of what is being removed and the light of truth shines, forcing all things to show themselves as they truly are! this is the great awakening and the grand process of ascension that is underway right now on planet earth the great masters have said, "now it is time to fully ascend so that you may know all things!" tonight we will tell you the rest of the story about humanity, earth, and the cosmos!

We will tell you what happened in earth's ancient past and we will shine a light on the current state of affairs of humanity's evolution and the grand ascension to the fifth-dimensional new earth. The data in this stream is lengthy and should be reviewed twice for it to be integrated. Read it slower the 2nd time and take notes on

The data points below. Some of the facts here are eye-opening, and it is advised that one look at the whole picture with an open mind! Be sure to do your research and truth-seeking on these subjects.

This channeled message is presented in the highest love for all humanity! Here are the amazing contents of this very important new light Forces message... begin transmission... as the guardians of planet earth and the beings here, we the Pleiadians have been watching over humanity's evolution and assisting mankind with the care of this planet for a very long time! Earth is a beautiful and special place in this cosmos and there is no other place like it! We created a divine plan for planet earth and set it in motion eons ago! We did not create the plan alone; in fact, you were personally involved in creating this divine plan the plan was to create a beautiful world on! Earth would function as an experiential ascension training ground to see how the beings that came here could evolve their way back up consciously to where they came from!

All the information about the game itself and the data collected from the experiences on earth was stored in the earth itself and hidden inside each player's body and the earth quickly evolved into a literal-living library for the entire cosmos! earth soon became known as the primary place in the universe for soul development and though you knew it would be a tough challenge to come here, there was still that excitement of it all so, from heaven to earth, you came down in all your glory you and billions of other higher beings which only knew higher-dimensional perfection began incarnating on the earth plane so you could experience the contrast of being

Physical! You came to earth with free will intent and you came with a plan! You planned everything that you would experience here and you planned how you would return one day to your higher state. Perfection! Since you were already perfect before you came to earth, you and the others had to devise a way so you would not be so aware of your perfection and would have to make it so you didn't know very much at least in the beginning! You and the others devised a way to limit access to your higher self-data and even most of your memories! You in essence turned down your conscious awareness to very low levels. You forgot who and what you truly are, and you forgot how to access the divine abilities that you have!

At that point, you entered a long unconscious state of amnesia and you were plunged into the dark with no information about what had happened or about much of anything else for that matter! This was the base starting point and the very first day of your great spiritual journey to planet earth which was in linear time, millions of years ago! when civilization first started on earth in ancient times it was very basic but eventually, it evolved into a more complex and advanced civilization these first beings of earth learned in time, the process of natural physical evolution takes a very, very long time on earth to occur and the process of soul evolution is another matter and takes much longer! The evolutionary project of planet earth was moving along with success and it seemed that no matter what challenge humanity met with, they would somehow always overcome it and evolve above it! Almost every challenge, that is! The rules of this earth game provided that everything was allowed as an obstacle to this higher ascension project, even natural earth disasters, and worse, cosmic level disasters! Five grand civilizations that existed before the great flood rose to incredible levels of technology and wisdom in their time however all five of these evolved earth races had one tragic thing in common: just as all of these civilizations were reaching the apex of their evolution a major cataclysmic event came along and completely wiped each one of them out!

All the progress, 99% of the civilization, all of its treasures, and all of its knowledge, instantly and wiped off the planet!

What's more, every time this planetary extinction happened, the amnesia factor got worse! of course, since these civilizations became extinct by cataclysms, the evolutionary work they were doing to move to the next highest dimension was cut short and according to the rules of their mission to earth, they had to come back and start again, multiple times!

It's important to say that each of these great civilizations that existed at different times was the same being and in fact 'it was ultimately only one great civilization with different names throughout prehistory and history! You were certainly there each time and every detailed memory of it all is still inside waiting to be remembered! In those ancient days, even though humanity was very advanced in each of these civilizations, it seemed they did not possess the ability, to prevent their destruction and extinction! The rules of the earth game say if you get knocked out of the game get up and keep going! Of course

, the resilience of the great beings that came to earth always Prevailed even if they had been knocked down-numerous times! We will remind you that you are still here today finishing what you started a long time ago! This time you finally make it to the finish line so be encouraged! When the Archeologists of today attempt to identify what happened to these ancient cultures they will look at the evidence and -say, "it looks like these ancient races were here one day and gone the next! it's as if they simply vanished without a trace in a single day!"

it is known on earth that most of these ancient cultures" stone structures, writings and creations were buried under 6 miles of earth sediment by the intense global Floods of each cataclysm! Before we transmit the important data markers in this transmission; we want to provide some basic background information about the event and the grand solar flash: what is the grand solar flash? the grand solar flash is a very high-magnitude, earth-directed solar flare known as a super flare which could register as an x-50 to x-100 or higher class n the x-ray scale!

An intense super flare from earth's sun would be witnessed by someone, on earth as a blinding flash' of magnetic, white light! the ancients called this cosmic flash of light many names Including Shamash and Samvartaka fire it is written about in every culture's ancient writings including the Vedas, The Sumerian tablets, biblical texts, Egyptian texts, and Mayan codex. the light emitted from this great cosmic flash is -exotic gamma-level light which resonates super high and is called the light of the stars! Gamma light is proven by earth science to instantaneously recode DNA, morphing it into a more complex and advanced state of functionality. The grand solar flash (the divine light) is the cosmic trigger and cause for what we simply called "the event" on planet earth the moment when this light impacts the surface of planet earth is called the compression breakthrough and this is the beginning of the earth event what is this earth event or simply, "the event"? It is a biological evolutionary event.

A DNA upgrade where the fifth strand of DNA is activated! The Vedas, says, "When the Samvartaka fire comes, rainbow. Colored clouds shall appear around the earth and people will attain their rainbow body-(a.k.a. the spirit light body). This is an instant transmutation and ascension to the 5th. A dimension that occurs in the twinkling of an eye! His event is a planetary liberation event. Since freedom is a fifth-dimensional energy, obviously the earth will experience an immediate planetary liberation at the time of this event! An event is an ascension event. it is an ascension/conscious event where the beings of earth expand their awareness to be able to perceive and exist in the fifth-dimensional reality on earth, this fifth-dimensional new earth is also called heaven and is a realm of only love, peace, perfect health, freedom, abundance, and all goodness! It's important to note that this heaven is not a place but à vibratory state of being or a resonance where a being will perceive a lighter nicer reality! This heaven is not far away up in the sky but all around you right now on earth, you would simply need your fifth strand of DNA active to be able to perceive it as the outward reality!

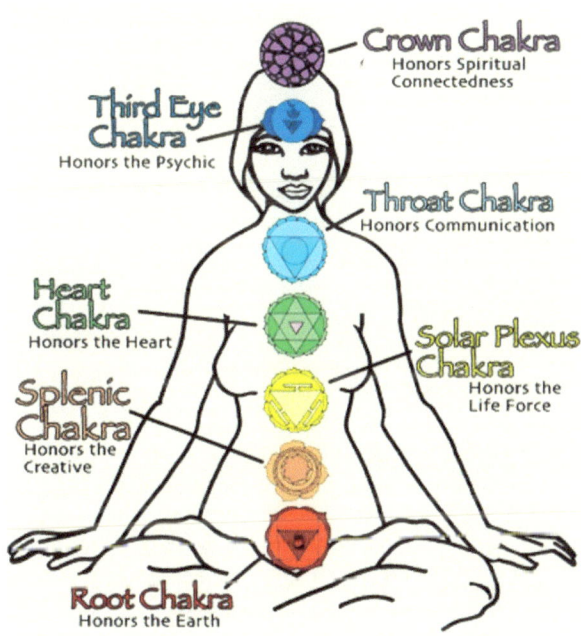

CHAPTER 4

DRACOS AND REPTILIANS LEARN THE HISTORY

Dracos And Reptiloids Draconoids or Dracos), like the Nagas, are descended from the Primordials and Black Archons, created personally by Yaldabaoth. These entities and powers are the foundation of the Grey eons, an integral part of the Universe that includes our 3D Earth. It is also the Supreme beings in which the madness of their Father, the Black Co-Creator of our Local Universe, has merged with the Light of Sophia, the World Mother, and Her son Yaltabaoth. Primogen Dracos and Nagas were born earlier than Man, raised by Yaltabaoth, but later than Perfect Man, brought into being by the Supreme Hierarch of Pleroma, who built eons and civilizations of Light. Draconoids and Nagas are very close genetically. There are even their hybrids, the Serpento-arachnoids. Both received possession of our Earth and completely dominated it, although they have different abodes in other places, for example, in the constellation of the Dragon and the Snake. It was before the appearance of man on our planet. When Adam was born and placed on Earth to "go forth and multiply", Dracos and Nagas, obeying the will of their Dark creator, went into the inner Earth, founding entire underground kingdoms in Agartha. They did not accept this situation and secretly decided to destroy mankind. But they did not intend to do it with their hands so that they would not be blamed for anything, but by Man himself. They built a whole system of his self-indulgence in men's sins and vices and self-the destruction that is in full effect today. The mechanism for the implementation of their plan was and is the visible and invisible power holders of this world. They are ruled by the external Gray civilizations, mostly reptilians. Everything in this world so far belongs to them. Of course, Co-Creators and the Higher Light Hierarchs helped humanity as much as they could, or otherwise, we would have been long gone, taking into account the power that wanted to destroy us. But now everything has changed dramatically. Nagas and Draco have lost their Dark creator and master, Yaldabaoth. He went to the Light Side and got a new name - Yaltabael. His former masterpieces" became property under abeyance".

They witnessed numerous Eliminations of Gray and Black beings. Co-Creators have put Dracos and Nagas before the choice: to undergo a conscious cleansing of karma and transformation to continue evolving in the United Light Family or to be zeroed as a counter-evolutionary force. From the beginning, Nagas were different. Some groups of them who were loyal to the man accepted the offer and even cooperate with Light warriors in many ops. The others remained on the Dark Side. This led to an intensified struggle within the race between the major clans for power and spheres of influence. Draco was also originally a constructive civilization. The Light of Sophia, which was partially transferred to them from her son Yaldabaoth, affected them. But later, the insanity gene of the Black Parents did its work. The race began to degenerate rapidly. As a result, there was a split, the division into two branches: Light and Dark. They did not have a middle one, Gray. On Earth, both groups of Dracos ruled from a long time ago - in the territory of modern China and other Asian countries.

There embodied the primary Dracos and dragon-like Intelligence forms. It is reflected in extant legends and artifacts Light Dracos are very wise and peaceful. The LFs' ground team interacted with them during one of its operations in China. Their planetary abode is in Beijing, in one of the halls in the Forbidden City, Gugong. The artifact of the Dracos is represented there by the Crystal of Celestial Purity, the combined energies of these entities' Luminosity. After jointly clearing the karma of the maternal Logos of the Light Dracos on the Altar of Heaven, the Lightwarriors received as a gift a Crystal copy which they sometimes use in their ops. Black Dracos are also rooted on Earth, and for a time two branches lived here in parallel.

Both are a higher form of Intelligence, having once possessed a single Monad and the bodies of its manifestation - the Logos and the Causal Body. After the split, each branch received half of the Monad. One was filled with Light, the other - with Darkness. As higher entities, each of them created their cosmic races. Black Dracos gave birth to many Intelligence forms similar to them but only in appearance.

They could not give them the Monads - only physical and Subtle Body That's how reptiles came about which is represented by many species. Only a few are on Earth - iguanas, lizards, crocodiles, chameleons, and turtles. Scientists also add snakes, though they are not reptiles, but the Nagas' creations. There are about 12,000 known subspecies of reptiles on Earth. Each of these reptiles, like almost all terrestrial Life forms, has a corresponding cosmo-civilization where they are dominant including a variety of Dinosaurs, also Draco's creatures. They developed all of them when there was no Man. And when they saw his form and potential, they decided to reproduce on his basis as a Reptilian, a hybrid of a Human and a Reptile. He, like others, "creations", too, had no Monad (Soul) -only a physical and Subtle Body. By the way, in Cosmos, only the lazy did not exploit the human image for their creations. There are known arachnid-humanoids (human hybrids with spiders), serpents-humanoids (hybrids with snakes), active-humanoids (hybrids with sea creatures, such as mermaids), man-monkeys, centaurs, bird-men, and many other hybrids. Different kinds of reptilian and reptiloid civilizations are very common in the Universe. Several of them are on our planet.

And everyone has interests and squabbles with each other over spheres of influence on "their" Earth....They came here a little later than the Nagas, even before Man, and for that reason consider this planet in no way ours, humans. This point is very important for all of us to understand why all these bacchanalian processes are going on around us right now. Reptiloids (repo-humanoids) were created imperfectly, flawed, and not self-sustainable.

They were abandoned by their creators to their fate, of self-organization, as they call it. It was, in fact, the wild survival. For it, reptiloid races do not have many options, mostly by correcting and improving their genetics. And there are not a lot of ways either theoretical research, experiments, crossbreeding, or hybridization with other, more perfect protein Life forms.

They have conducted and are conducting extensive crossbreeding with various species, to bring genetic material into their genome that can enhance it. Their main problem is an acute lack of Lifeforce. The energy received at birth is enough for a very short time, and the "battery" discharges quickly.

A separate area is an experimentation with crossbreeding with men, introducing human genetic material into their DNA. The physical body of any earthling has a protein basis. Our body consists of DNA segments and genes brought into it by space donors. Among them were Pleiadeans and 32 main "parents", as well as others, more than a hundred in total. Such genetic mix, by the principle of large-knot assembly (like cars in a factory), is the warp and woof of our physical bodies. Of course, the question of the interaction of different genetic blocks and units brought by different civilizations leaves much to be desired. A special place in our genetics is occupied by reptilian segments, i.e. sections of the interaction of different genetic blocks and units brought by different civilizations leave much to be desired.

A special place in our genetics is occupied by reptilian segments, i.e. sections of DNA and groups of genes brought in by reptilians. On completely legitimate grounds, they are also among our genetic godfathers. Modern science denies it. Although how can it not deny it? Then it would have to admit that man descended from a reptile, and not from an ape, as they claim until now. It is a fact that a human being has rudiments, for example, the coccyx, which is a degenerated queue. And at the initial stages of intrauterine development of the human embryo, all have a tail. Gills were also thought to be present, but scientists have now disproved them. What used to be thought to be gills turned out to be only folds of tissue in the human embryo – the precursors of the head and neck. Since then, these folds have been called "gill arches". Although it is more correct to call them "visceral" because internal organs are formed from them. Gill slits, same as they are in cold-blooded animals, the human embryos are not formed. Reptile insertions in human genetics are an objective reality. They give us strong innate immunity and increase regenerative capabilities, i.e. our survivability.

For example, severed limbs in some reptiles regenerate and grow back. That was supposed to be with humans as it was in the last Satya Yuga. At present, a very serious disagreement arose between the reptiloid clans controlling Earth which led to a split. Some disobeyed the Council of Elders, which decided to peacefully evacuate the entire race from Earth.

The rebels represent an influential group of irreconcilables who refused to leave Earth and give it to earthlings. They put skin in the game in an attempt, and now try to reduce the Earth's population as retaliation and bargaining. They will not start a new "hot" world war, for it is mutual annihilation Killing humanity through the propaganda of violence, drugs, unhealthy lifestyles, and diet, GMOs work too slowly. The introduction of degenerate models and a system of values at odds with natural human nature does not meet expectations.

There remain viruses. The whole current campaign is planned and billions of dollars are being thrown into it now, pumping trillions out of it at the same time... But even this is not yielding the expected results. Galactic Committee suspects that the reptiloids, by introducing their genetics into the human DNA Matrix, may have installed a time bomb into it.

Galacom does not exclude that some vaccines may carry an alien genetic insertion that, through a key put in, could trigger the repo program in our body. Most likely, our tails won't start to grow (though, who knows....). But if the reptilian genes are responsible for our immunity, we can assume that it could be influenced by them. For example, just turn it off. What the AIDS virus does, a masterpiece of Black geneticists. The situation is now under the constant tight control of the Higher Light Hierarchy and Galactic Committee. For now, it remains difficult. Against the background of Galacom withdrawing the energies of the old 3D Matrix, de-energizing it, a colossal drain on humanity's vital force continues at the same time. How did it become possible?

CHAPTER 5

ELON MUSK IS TRYING TO TAKE OVER THE WORLD AS A DRACO REPTILIAN

The Power of Ra, The Galactic Confederation, and why the Great Experiment on Earth was created (Part 1) The first humans were Lyran and Sirian in our universal matrix bubble. Conflict broke out in the Cradle of Lyra the Lyran constellation) between the negatively polarised Orion races and the Lyrans. This led to heavy and long-drawn-out conflict which we know as the Orien wars (which is what the Star Wars movie series is about The Orions/Draco invaded the Lyran system corrupting their social memory complex and in the process, 50 million souls were lost in the destruction of, 3 planets (Bila, Teka, and Merok). The negative Orion/Draco factions sided with the dark (black sun) Empire which was 95% oriented towards the service to self-polarity whilst the Lyran/ Sirians followed the Law of One and the rays (Ray - Ra) of light that were of service to others/ unity consciousness. Christ is a shortened version of Christos that translates as man and human which means the light of man. Man is Ra; the pathway to the light. The universal matrix conforms to the light cube (Ra) and dark cube (Satan) to form the YHVH duality matrix, The YHVH Metatronic grid gives beings the choice to choose their consciousness via the flower of life sacred geometry held within our DNA blueprint.

In gematria YHVH equates to 26 (Y = 10 H = 5 V = 6 H = 5) as does man (m = 1 a = 12 n = 13). 26 divided into the two polarities gives you 13. The 13th portal is the gateway back to either the light of God (golden dawn via the heart) or the false god (of the gliphoth) depending on what path you choose to walk in your evolutionary soul journey. 26 condensed down in numerology gives you 8 by adding the 2 and 6 together.

8 is the symbol for infinity which connects to the 8th-dimensional portal of Orion that holds the library of all things infinite torus of the akashic records data field) and connects to the black hole void portal of god "Hunab Ku". 8 also aligns to the 8 points that connect up to the light and dark 3D cube of our reality (Kabbalah tree of life/death) that holds our vibrations through the 3 dimensions of height, width, and depth. The 144 vibrations within Metatron's cube contain the full spectrum of light and dark that can be separated by the 4 elements and pillars (earth, water, fire, and air) of the square shape geometry (2D) to use for positive or negative purposes, Light cube = 4, dark cube a 4 connected to the 1 infinitive creator through the ether = 144. 144 divided by 2 = 72. 72 light vibrations (god of light 742-= 9. 9 the dimension of God and the higher self/higher mind) and 72 dark vibrations (false god self and ego lower self/lower mind). The Dark Orion Empire's commanding forces were known as Sith Lords or dominator-victimizers. The Orion Resistance known as the Black: League fought against the Empire but many of them fell

to darkness or became enslaved by the dominators. Some of the members of the Resistance were Ray (Ra) Masters of the light that held potent dragon energy (Kumara Dragons) but still managed to become corrupted through killing in dualistic battles; thus heavily shifting their vibrations to alter their states of consciousness towards the negative polarity.

The Dark Orion Empire used victimizer mind technology also referred to as Armageddon software to hijack beings of light, submitting them to darkness and slavery through deep fear holographic implants/destructive false memories seeded in the unconscious mind. The Draco reptilians and their Orion allies on Regal used their advanced war weaponry and mind control technology to infiltrate and enslave native Inhabitants in 21-star systems. The Lyrans and Vegans were a peaceful human and feline civilization that developed agriculture on several planets and thrived in their service to others mentality.

Tiny wasn't expecting the attacks from the reptilians but even whilst unprepared, still they fought back, Some of the w-is led to a truce between certain reptilian and human/feline groups which saw them cohabitate with one another peacefully and even started interbreeding. This is how I believe the cat/feline species got the reptilian eye genetics, as a result of this hybridization.

These were the reptilian factions that managed to break away from the Empire and choose their path (Kalask and Morkul). The tyranny of the Orion onslaught grew too powerful for the Lyrans to handle and so they fled Lyra to colonize new human civilizations on other planets such as Arcturus, the Pleiades, Cygnus Alpha, Antares, Cassiopeia, Alpha Centauri and

Andromeda to name a few. Humans spread across 110 different star systems, developing their spiritual practices and technologies in their new evolutionary cycles, The original Lyran refugees fled to the Zenetae star system in the Andromedan Galaxy.

Lyra is the 12th Gate that connects directly to Andromeda. When Lyra was taken over and partly destroyed, in the process of its fall, its natural Kryst (christ) codes and crystal architecture. of eternal living, the light became reversed and locked into the Milky way system to feed the black cube matrix and negative entities. The Metatronic collective tried to repair this distortion but sadly was unsuccessful and got absorbed into the AI matrix. This only made the black hole to Abaddon more powerful for the dark entities to maneuver in and pass through to our universe and strengthen, the dark alliances of Orion and its Empire, Luckily now, this is changing thanks to the Aquaferion Shield collective consisting of 12 Andromedan tribes who have energetically connected the 12 pillar halls of Zion with the help of the 12 children of the Law of One (currently incarnated in human form on the belt that is unblocking the 8th portal access to Orion allowing for the 12th portal of the planetary gates and the Aquaferion Shield kundalini energy to flow through to us to give us new life forces.

This includes unblocking negative distortions in our pineal gland, pituitary glands, hypothalamus, and other parts of the brain which were previously keeping us 'asleep' and feeding our life forces to the negative astral entities in the 4th dimension. This is all part of retrieving the lost 12 DNA strands in 12 trees of life grid templates. Elon Musk betrayed the light forces in Andromeda by switching sides; assisting the Draco reptilians in the Al Abaddon infiltration takeover. This is why in his current incarnation he has disguised some of his Space X rocket activity as 'space exploration ventures' when in fact he is sending war weapons targeted at Andromeda to disrupt the Aquaferion Shield network. Their work is blocking the path for Musk to collect more transhuman and artificial grid AI technology from his reptilian allies on Mars to slow down the 5D transition and take as many souls with him before the final transition takes place. The 110 human colonies that branched off from Lyra joined together to create the Galactic Federation of Light and learned as a collective unit how to repel and diffuse reptilian hostility and invasions. They are assisting in allowing these new positive energies to flow through the portals without interference. The darkness is now trapped and the new blueprint is locked in place, Channel by king kenkeenfior from The Nibiru star system.

BE PREPARED FOR A LIFE CHANGE

If you enjoyed the content in this book purchase the spiritual pillar of life, unlock the gateway to your soul second edition and continue reading.

For booking and speaking engagements
call this number 470-861-6114

Or email us unlockthegatewaytoyoursoul@gmail.com

For booking Michael Alan Sheffield or
if you would like a one-on-one

Spiritual Awakening session!

www.ingramcontent.com/pod-product-compliance
Lightning Source LLC
Chambersburg PA
CBHW042324150426
43192CB00001B/40